MW00874269

The Doctor From

Hell

The True Story of Harold Shipman One of Britain's Most Prolific Serial Killer With an Estimated 218 Victims

True Crime Explicit Volume 7

Genoveva Ortiz, True Crime Seven

TRUE CRIME 7

ISBN: 9798840508602

Table of Contents

Introduction...11

I A Normal Boyhood..13

II Life as a Medical Student.................................20

III First Crimes..27

IV Drug Troubles...36

V Getting Off Easy...53

VI The Private Practice...59

VII The Best Doctor in Hyde................................70

VIII Mrs. Grundy...79

IX A New Investigation...85

X Odds Stacked Against Him................................90

XI The Doctor's Death...96

Conclusion...99

References *101*

Acknowledgements *103*

About True Crime Seven *121*

Explore the Stories of

The Murderous Minds

A Note

From True Crime Seven

Hi there!

Thank you so much for picking up our book! Before you continue your exploration into the dark world of killers, we wanted to take a quick moment to explain the purpose of our books.

Our goal is to simply explore and tell the stories of various killers in the world: from unknown murderers to infamous serial killers. Our books are designed to be short and inclusive; we want to tell a good scary true story that anyone can enjoy regardless of their reading level.

That is why you won't see too many fancy words or complicated sentence structures in our books. Also, to prevent typical cut and dry style of true crime books, we try to keep the narrative easy to follow while incorporating fiction style storytelling. As to information, we often find ourselves with too little or too much. So, in terms of research material and content, we always try to include what further helps the story of the killer.

Lastly, we want to acknowledge that, much like history, true crime is a subject that can often be interpreted differently. Depending on the topic and your upbringing, you might agree or disagree with how we present a story. We understand disagreements are inevitable. That is why we added this note so hopefully it can help you better understand our position and goal.

Now without further ado, let the exploration to the dark begin!

Introduction

HE WAS LIKE A FAVORITE UNCLE. THEY SAID HE always made time for his patients, even if it was just to chat. He remembered the little things about their lives they thought no one cared about. He made them feel safe and cared for. He was the shining example of what a good doctor ought to be.

He was also the most prolific serial killer in modern history.

There are people in our lives we feel we should always be able to trust. They care for us and keep us healthy; thus, we believe they have our best interests at heart. Why else would they place themselves in these positions of power if they did not?

Unfortunately, humans are not always so simple – or kind. Sometimes the people we trust the most are the ones who can betray us the worst. That was certainly true for the citizens of Hyde, a small town in Manchester, England, from the early 1980s to the late 90s. No one had any idea what Doctor Harold Shipman, known as Fred to his few friends, was really like.

His was a story so outrageous that it was almost unbelievable. After all, there were no signs that anything was wrong with the man. He was well-respected, even doing charity work during the rare times he was free. But beneath this genial façade lurked a monster unlike any the world has ever known.

This book will examine the life and crimes of England's killer doctor and try to make sense of how he almost got away with murder.

I

A Normal Boyhood

HAROLD FREDERICK SHIPMAN WAS BORN ON January 14th, 1946, in Nottingham, England, eight months after Germany surrendered to the Allied Forces and brought an end to the bloodiest conflict of the century. It was a particularly special time to be born; with the end of the Second World War came a population boom in the form of celebration babies, marking a hopeful new beginning for a nation that had been ravaged for so long by destruction. This was partly why young Harold Shipman, the second child born to working-class parents Harold and Vera, was, by all accounts, their favorite. His sister, Pauline, was his senior by seven years, and his brother, Clive, was his junior by four. While his siblings seemed doomed to a life of mediocrity, Harold gained a reputation as the clever one in the family. From boyhood, he was convinced by his mother that he was destined for great things.

Both the war and their familial backgrounds – Vera and the elder Harold were descended from manual laborers – instilled in the Shipman parents a desire to give their children the best lives they could afford. That their older boy showed the most potential meant that much of the family's hopes were pinned almost entirely on the boy's shoulders. Though the fear of failure was great, it surprisingly did not seem to create any feelings of resentment between them. On the contrary, their bond only seemed to grow stronger as Harold reached adolescence.

While not much is known about young Harold's relationship with his father, it was no secret that he remained very close to his mother for the rest of his childhood. This was less by his own choice than by his mother's insistence. Vera was said to have been overprotective and somewhat overbearing when it came to her favorite son. From the clothes he wore to the friends he was allowed to make at school, Vera always made sure he made the proper choices.

But she took genuine joy in her role as a housewife. The Shipman home, from what the few outsiders who were invited in can remember, was always a spotless place. Her children were polite, well-behaved, and almost always kept at home. It was something that other people admired her for, though they also found the Shipmans somewhat odd. Hannah Cutler, a neighbor who lived in the area during Harold's youth, recounted

"The family were rather insular, but I knew them well because I lived opposite. I've known the children since they were little. They never mixed in with the other kids, they didn't play in the street, and when they came home from school, they stayed in the house. I think Harold and Vera wanted them to be different: they didn't want them to be like other kids on the estate; they wanted something better for them. In a way, they were investing in their children."

Vera's efforts to shape her son's identity proved largely successful. While he was still a schoolboy, Harold – known as "Freddy or Fred" by his peers – developed a rather arrogant personality that would remain throughout his life. This seemingly extended even to his manner of dress; while other children wore casual clothing outside of school, Vera kept Harold prim and proper at all times, and her idea of "well dressed" meant a bowtie and waistcoat, no matter the occasion.

His youth was not entirely solitary. He was close to his siblings, especially Pauline. A few houses away on their street in the Edwards Lane estate lived a boy named Alan Goddard. Just a few months younger than Harold, Alan attended the Buford Infants School – in the United Kingdom, children attend infants school from ages four to seven and could be seen as a partial equivalent to elementary school in the United States – alongside him. Goddard would recall seeing Harold often during the short walk home during those early childhood days, and soon the boys became friends.

The friendship would continue as they grew older. The unexpected population boom of post-war celebration babies meant that the local junior school, Whitemoor, was unprepared for so many new pupils. As a result, the boys stayed at Buford for an additional year before they were allowed to take double-decker buses to and from Whitemoor – a first taste of independence for young Fred.

He was said to have been a good, though not spectacular, student. Little of note happened during most of his time at

Whitemoor aside from a struggle with left-handedness – something which, in those days, was seen as a malady to be fixed, which had a profoundly negative effect on the psyches of left-handed children. He did, however, discover a passion for sports, namely stoolball, a local sport similar to cricket and baseball. It was on the field that a more outgoing, though aggressive, side of his personality broke loose.

He studied hard and got good grades. Along with stoolball, Harold excelled at football – the term for soccer in the United Kingdom – and rugby. Despite these accomplishments, his mother's high standards and his own elitism made it difficult for him to make friends. Even throughout his junior school years, the boy was seen as a loner by others.

After finishing his primary education at around eleven years old, Fred was accepted into High Pavement Grammar School in September 1957. It was just what his mother had been hoping for. Founded near the end of the 16th century, High Pavement was a prestigious, all-boys school considered to be the best in the area.

Unfortunately, his time there was not what he and his family had been expecting. While he had been considered an exceptional student before, the other boys at this new school were also some of the best in their class. For the first time in his life, Harold was not special, and the feeling of being lost within a crowd made him deeply unhappy.

When one thinks of a serial killer's life, one might typically assume that they must have suffered a great deal of emotional trauma to become someone capable of the most depraved acts. This is not a baseless assumption; countless true crime books and documentaries are filled with stories of killers who endured unimaginable suffering and abuse in their early lives. Also common are childhood injuries to the brain and family histories of mental illness. Harold Shipman, however, experienced none of these and, by all accounts, had a happy childhood.

However, things would take an unfortunate turn when he was around seventeen years old. At this time, his beloved mother fell ill and was diagnosed with terminal lung cancer.

Fred watched the once vibrant woman rapidly become a shell of her former self. With his father and sister at work and Clive at school, he readily became her caretaker. Vera's illness pulled the two to grow closer as the already-solitary teenager took it upon himself to come home from school straight away each day in order to be by her side. These afternoons spent drinking tea and waiting for the doctor were as much a comfort to him as they were to Vera, though the memory of them would always be tainted by tragedy.

Hospice care was much less common in that era, which meant that Vera would remain at home, confined to her bed, till the end. Her condition continued to deteriorate, and she grew weak and emaciated. Soon, little else could be done for her aside from easing her suffering. The only thing that could allay her unending pain was morphine, which Harold watched get administered to his mother via injection whenever the family's doctor made house calls.

This act fascinated the teenager. One moment, his mother was ailing, and the next, she was her old self again. The fact that the opiate was so fast-acting was not lost on him, either.

On Friday, June 21, 1963, Vera Shipman succumbed to her disease at only forty-three years old. While the rest of the family mourned in the traditional way, Fred spent the weekend running nonstop in the pouring rain, intentionally exhausting himself. By Monday, he was back at school, and his reaction puzzled his few friends. People would note that Fred appeared, on the surface, almost entirely unaffected.

When a classmate asked about his weekend, all he said was, "My mum died." No one at school even knew Vera had been ill.

His mother's death was no doubt a turning point in his life. Although Harold had previously shown no interest in studying medicine, Vera's death seemed to trigger in him a deep interest in the field, and he decided that he wanted to become a doctor. It would be a long and difficult road to take, but it would be worth it if he could do for others what the family doctor had done for his mother.

There were other reasons too, but those were far less noble.

II

Life as a Medical Student

SHIPMAN FINISHED GRAMMAR SCHOOL IN 1964, around a year after his mother's death. The loss had deeply affected him, but Shipman had never been the kind of person to reveal too much of his emotions. Instead, he buried himself in his studies, fully intent on becoming a doctor someday.

The road to medical school was not the straight path he had been anticipating. He failed to gain acceptance on his first try, and it would not be until a few attempts later, September 1965, that Shipman finally got into Leeds University Medical School.

He was eager to leave home, which he was able to do thanks to a student grant he received. Though he loved his remaining family, the death of his beloved mother made staying in his childhood home almost unbearable.

It was also around this time that Shipman met the girl who would later become his wife.

During his commute to school, he often took a bus that was also frequented by seventeen-year-old Primrose Oxtoby, a window dresser at a nearby department store. Shipman quickly took notice of her, which was something that had never happened to the girl before.

Primrose was likely the kind of girl that Vera Shipman would have never approved of. She lacked the sophistication and sense of elitism that had been groomed into Shipman since boyhood, despite their upbringings being more similar than not.

Like the Shipmans, the Oxtobys came from humble, working-class backgrounds. Her father, George, was a farmhand, while her mother, Edna, was a domestic servant until the birth of her first daughter in 1936. Both were devout Methodists, but Edna was the one with a real zeal for religion and named their elder daughter Mary.

Primrose was the youngest child by thirteen years. Her parents, who had been hoping for a son, were disappointed in getting a daughter, something the girl seemed to have picked up on at an early age. Indeed, much of her life before encountering Harold had been spent feeling like an outsider, always unwanted in favor of someone prettier or more charming. Her few friends rarely came around as they were fearful of the strict Mrs. Oxtoby, and she was not allowed to go out dancing or to movies like other teenagers. Una Ripley, her childhood friend, recalled:

"I was her best pal, but she wasn't mine because she could never go out with us. My mother thought it was terrible the way her parents controlled her. But she never complained. She never talked about clothes or makeup – she seemed to accept that she couldn't have them."

Unfortunately, for the old-fashioned Oxtobys, it was the Swinging Sixties, and teen rebellion was very much en vogue. It was the era of rock 'n' roll and miniskirts – something that Primrose, who bore an unflattering bowl cut, was well aware of. The other girls at school started getting boyfriends, while the kindest thing most of her male peers would say about her was that she was "unobtrusive."

Some sources describe Primrose as "barely literate," while others describe her as having been bright in her youth. Whichever the case, Primrose did have an artistic side. She was fond of painting, and after she finished secondary school, she briefly studied art and design. She was only sixteen by the time all her education was over, but it was enough to land her a decent job as a window dresser.

Employment gave her a taste of the freedom she had never had. She had her own money to spend as she pleased – though she gave the majority of it to her parents to help out. The bus ride to Leeds exposed her to new kinds of people and places, including pubs. Now that she knew what life could be like for other girls, it was impossible for her to fit back into the role her parents made for her.

It is crucial to understand Primose's early life if we want to explain how she ended up the way she did – devoted to a serial killer and lost in her own denial. While her parents' strictness was born out of love and a desire for her to have a better life than they had, it clearly suffocated the lonely girl. Had they not been so traditional, she might not have rebelled as hard as she did.

For reasons that are unclear, Edna was wary of her future son-in-law from the start, and to her dismay, Primrose was immediately drawn to Shipman. Despite their differences in personality, the pair hit it off. Her friends were happy for her. They had their first date at a local coffee shop and soon began a relationship.

Shipman was just as glad to have found a partner as Primrose was. Having attended an all-boys school for so long, coupled with his sometimes off-putting personality, Harold had no experience with girls. In his grammar school days, during one of the rare times he attended a dance, he brought his sister, Pauline, along as his date.

But things would get serious far sooner than either of them liked. They were only together for a few months when Primrose became pregnant. Shipman was nineteen years old, and Primrose was just seventeen.

If Primrose's relationship with her parents was tense before, it all but broke when the news of her pregnancy reached them. The scandalized Oxtobys demanded that Shipman, irrespective of their dislike of him, marry their daughter to make the situation right. The young couple did just that, having a small court ceremony on

November 5, 1966, attended by none of their friends. Still, the damage was done. Primrose's parents never forgave her.

Her family's ire mattered little to Primrose at the time. At last, it appeared that she had found someone who loved her as she was; in turn, she adored Shipman.

But as happy as they were, reality would soon set in; there were logistical issues to think about. For one, Shipman did not have a place of his own. Leeds University students typically lived in the residence halls provided by the school, but once again, the post-war population boom presented unforeseen predicaments. University lodging filled up quickly, and those left over, such as Shipman, were sent to live with preapproved families. When he and Primrose met, he and another medical student were housed with an older couple. Additionally, his student stipend was only around three hundred forty pounds – a sum equivalent to just over six thousand pounds or seventy-three hundred American dollars today.

Shipman had a hectic schedule, full of early-morning lectures, labs, and work, and had little time for his new wife. As a result, Primrose spent the remainder of her pregnancy back at her parents' home. On Valentine's Day 1967, just four months after their wedding, she gave birth to a daughter named Sarah Rosemary.

It would be a few more months before Shipman and Primrose reunited, this time at a rented apartment close to the University. Primrose dedicated herself to becoming the perfect wife and mother and, by all accounts, appeared to have succeeded in her goal, at least in those first years together. Her new husband, on the other hand, was not doing nearly as well.

"I was a bright boy," he confided in a co-worker. "I should have known better, shouldn't have I?"

It is not believed that Shipman held any resentment toward his new family, though he sometimes seemed to express regret. Would he have settled down with Primrose if he had not gotten her pregnant? Those who knew Shipman at the time seemed to believe not. There was a sense that he was missing out on the exciting days of his youth: partying, going out to clubs, and meeting girls.

For as much as the couple got along, Shipman struggled with balancing marriage, fatherhood, and medical school. One of the few ways he had to soothe his stress was through football, which he still excelled at. It was also, unsurprisingly, one of the few things he had left that allowed him to feel superior over others.

The couple scraped by for the next three years. Shipman graduated from Leeds Medical School in 1970, at the age of twenty-four. From there, he became a pre-registration house officer at Pontefract General Infirmary in the county of Yorkshire. This position is perhaps most similar to what is commonly called a residency in the United States. Here, Shipman would remain for the next few years, working and studying without incident- for the most part.

III

First Crimes

IF MEDICAL SCHOOL HAD BEEN HARD, SHIPMAN'S first year as a junior houseman at Pontefract General Infirmary was no easier. The initial six months were mostly comprised of medical work, while the latter six were surgical. It was undoubtedly a stressful time, but Shipman's supervisors considered him to be hard-working and bright. This is perhaps partly why he decided to remain at Pontefract for almost three more years after the mandatory period.

Between work and further studying, Shipman and his wife Primrose found the time to welcome a second child into their family. Christopher Fredrick Shipman was born April 21, 1971. By then, the Shipmans had moved into a small, brick house on the grounds at Pontefract. The cheap rent and proximity to work gave Shipman more time for studying, and he would soon acquire a diploma in child health as well as one in obstetrics and gynecology.

Money was less of an issue now than it had been during his time at Leeds, but funds were still tight. A demanding schedule caused him to become more asocial, very rarely spending time on his own. Whenever other local hospitals had staff shortages, he would fill in for them to earn extra cash.

Shipman had never been the kind of person who let his emotions show. On the outside, he was extremely confident in his medical knowledge and skills – some co-workers would say to the point of arrogance. To staff at the hospital, he seemed to be in constant competition with the other doctors. Repressing his emotions helped him feel that he was in complete control, something he always sought. There is no doubt, however, that he was quickly reaching his limit. Perhaps it is no coincidence that Shipman's darker urges were beginning to show around this time.

In 1972, a young nurse would experience some of this darkness during a night shift and be scarred for decades to come.

Sandra Whitehead was only eighteen years old and technically still a student when she came to work at Pontefract alongside Shipman. It was an already difficult job made worse by the amount of tragedy she saw in terms of patient deaths. One particular evening made her question if she was even cut out for the job to begin with.

They were working in a medical ward with thirty-two beds. That night there were three patient deaths, all of them older widows: seventy-four-year-old Agnes Davidson, seventy-four-year-old Elizabeth Thwaites, and eighty-year-old Alice Smith. It was a peculiarly high number of deaths for one shift in a ward that size, and Whitehead could not help but feel that something was wrong. After all, she had tended to those women before. They were elderly and sick, but none had been so ill that they were close to death. Stranger still, there had been empty injection packets by all three of their beds – but what had they needed injections for?

It made her realize that this one night had not been the only time. There had been mysterious needles before, but she was only now noticing an unsettling pattern.

But perhaps most puzzling of all had been how Shipman acted about the whole thing. He was behaving casually, almost aloof, despite all three women dying after he had visited their rooms. Whitehead was understandably suspicious, but she was also inexperienced. Figuring that Shipman likely knew better than her, she ultimately decided against reporting the incidents.

This was a decision that would haunt her for decades to come. It would not be until 1999, when Harold Shipman was in the news for being accused of murder, that she realized the magnitude of what had happened. In her own words, it felt "like hitting a brick wall at sixty miles per hour."

Another incident that occurred around the same time would also be shrouded in secrecy for several years. That November, four-year-old Susie Garfitt was placed under Shipman's care. Unlike the previous three women, it was expected that the little girl – a half-blind, mute quadriplegic with cerebral palsy who was suffering from severe pneumonia – would die sooner rather than later.

Susie was in pain and not getting better. Shipman told the girl's mother that it would be "unkind" to prolong her suffering.

"Please be kind to her," said the distraught mother before bending over the bed to give her daughter one last kiss. She said a quiet prayer before leaving the room to get a much-needed cup of tea.

It is vital to note that, despite the ambiguity of her statement, Mrs. Garfitt never gave the doctor explicit permission to do anything but help little Susie stay alive. And yet, when Mrs. Garfitt returned from her tea, she found the door to her daughter's room closed.

"I think that by these comments the doctor wanted to see whether I wanted to keep Susie alive at all costs," Mrs. Garfitt would later recall.

Just moments later, a nurse came to give her tragic news as well as condolences; Susie had died during the short time her mother had been away.

Mrs. Garfitt could do nothing but stand there, staring in shock at the closed door. It had all happened so soon – too soon. She hadn't even gotten the chance to say goodbye.

Susie Garfitt is only sometimes considered Shipman's first official victim. Indeed, the girl was not a coincidence, in more ways than one, regarding the people who died at his hands. Not only was she actually critically ill, but she was also a child – his only child victim. His next youngest victim was forty-one years old. Ultimately, The Shipman Inquiry would determine that while Susie's death was certainly suspicious, there simply was not enough evidence of murder for Shipman to be charged for it.

Had the death of Susie Garfitt been practice for all the terrible deeds that Shipman was about to commit? Or was it simply a sad coincidence? It seems that we will likely never know for sure. No doubt, some pieces of important information were lost within the decades before a real investigation could take place.

This loss of critical medical records would have disastrous consequences down the line: pinpointing Shipman's actual first victim and what year he began killing was now impossible. For a long time, police did not take into consideration Shipman's time at Pontefract when investigating his crimes. Out of the one hundred thirty-seven deaths he was present for, records only survived for around twenty-eight of them, many of those incomplete.

So, who was really the first patient he murdered? Brian Whittle, who authored, "*Harold Shipman: Prescription for Murder*" alongside Jean Ritchie, estimates that he likely began killing just six months into his junior housemanship at Pontefract. Whittle writes:

"His first six months at the hospital, during his pre-registration year, were spent on the surgical wards. Of the fourteen deaths he certified during this period, all were almost certainly natural deaths. There are limited records available, but there are no suspicious circumstances, and as a very junior doctor Shipman would have been under close supervision. He moved to the medical wards in February 1971, and it is here, while he was still not a fully registered doctor, that he may have killed his first victims. There were twenty-five deaths involving him during this period, and four of them have been classified as raising 'cause for some suspicion...' What is clear, though, from these subsequent deaths in the hospital, is that his killing began as a means of hastening deaths that were already on their way."

Considering the limited information available on these patients, who were sixty-seven-year-old Margaret Thompson, sixty-two-year-old Wilfred Sanderson, sixty-year-old Ethel Fallon, and forty-nine-year-old Edith Swift, it is not difficult to come to the conclusion that Shipman could have killed them as a means of easing their suffering. Of the four, two suffered from serious

37

conditions, such as a massive stroke and an inoperable brain tumor. This would also fit the pattern of what would later happen with Susie Garfitt.

However, details surrounding the rest of the deaths at Pontefract paint a more sinister picture. Shipman was starting to show a troubling fixation on drugs. On one occasion, he administered an exorbitant amount of sedative to a teenager only needing stitches for an injury and reportedly kept giving the drug even when told to stop. He was not only present when a patient died – something quite rare for other doctors – but was also frequently alone with them. More and more patients began dying of heart problems or strokes, and many died in the evenings – during the times when hospitals are far less busy and have fewer people to notice when something is amiss.

Patients that annoyed Shipman also had a tendency to perish before their time. One example of this was fifty-four-year-old Thomas Cullumbine, a former bus driver whose chronic lung issues forced him into an early retirement. It was said that Cullumbine hated doctors and never listened to any health advice he was given, no matter how sound. He struggled to breathe but still asked around the ward for cigarettes despite the doctor's orders.

This blatant disregard for his instructions no doubt infuriated Shipman. That April, when Cullumbine's health took a turn for the worse and he was readmitted to the hospital, Shipman convinced his family to go home instead of spending the night at his bedside. When Cullumbine grew weaker, Shipman did not bother calling for a nurse. He prescribed and administered morphine to the ailing man, with seemingly no reason for it. By the morning, the patient was dead.

One must wonder. Did the fact that Shipman would appear to be so beloved in the following decades have anything to do with him murdering anyone who complained – or criticized him?

It is easy for us to look back now and see the pattern of an emerging killer, but Shipman began his medical career at the end of an era in the United Kingdom where there simply were not enough doctors to go around. Shipman's hard-working nature was seen as a credit to his ability as a doctor. Other hospital staff certainly seemed to think highly of him, with some saying that they would hope Shipman would be on duty if any of their children ever fell ill.

Nobody had any idea that a monster roamed the halls at Pontefract, taking almost as many lives as he was saving.

In the meantime, Shipman's life would continue as normal.

By 1974, he was a fully registered doctor and held medical diplomas in child health, obstetrics, and gynecology. That same year, he was finally ready to work on his own. He applied to a position advertised in a medical journal at another medical center in West Yorkshire.

Shipman took the job and again quickly proved himself as a doctor. His life, it appeared, was looking up again, and everyone was none the wiser.

IV

Drug Troubles

I N 1974, HAROLD SHIPMAN BEGAN HIS FIRST JOB AS a fully registered doctor at the Abraham Ormerod Medical Centre in Todmorden, West Yorkshire, first as an assistant general practitioner and then as a full junior partner. Shipman immediately proved to be an excellent fit for the position; not only did he have a surprisingly warm bedside manner with the patients, but he was also more technologically literate than the other partners. Shipman's technological prowess extended beyond patient record-keeping and to the actual procedures the doctors performed. The fact that he had graduated recently meant he was far more up-to-date with the latest science.

The senior partners, Dr. Michael Grieve, Dr. John Dacre, and Dr. David Bunn, were especially glad to have Shipman join their ranks. Todmorden had a population of around seventeen thousand, and Ormerod Medical Centre, one of the two practices in the area, was said to sometimes treat more than half of that number.

"We were at rock bottom," explained Dr. Grieve. "We really saw him as our savior."

Because of this, he was instantly well-liked, and he no doubt relished the positive attention. For the first time in his life, Shipman's personality began to change. Where he was described as a sullen loner with few close friends before, he now became far more sociable, almost friendly. This soon led to him becoming a favorite of many of his patients, who loved that he always took the time to sit with them and really listen to their concerns during what were typically very short appointments.

Shipman's good reputation soon spread to the rest of the community. He began charity work alongside Dr. Grieve on weekends when he joined the Rochdale Canal Society. His involvement meant spending his precious spare time doing hard labor, digging the mud out of the old canal bed, hoping to open up the Rochdale Canal again. Primrose also got involved, teaming up with the other wives to feed the volunteers.

There was no question about Shipman's competency as a doctor among his peers. Still, the lower staff at Ormerod Medical Centre, such as nurses and receptionists, were less convinced of his supposed good nature. While he was a generally pleasant person to work with, he still had a short temper, particularly when it came to the shortcomings of anyone he considered to be beneath him.

In his own mind, Shipman's ideas and way of doing things were always correct. Any suggestions to the contrary were foolish, even deserving of ridicule. Those brave enough to speak their mind around him often found the doctor shouting and berating them, sometimes calling them stupid. It was his go-to insult, and he seemed to take a sort of twisted pleasure in making other people feel small.

Such outbursts were tolerated because of his skill and popularity. However, just a few months after his start at the center, a tragic incident would occur that seemed to push Shipman over the edge.

It was August of 1974. Shipman was tending to Susan Orlinski, a young woman in labor with her first child, a boy she and her husband, Mark, would name Christian. Susan, of course, was in a great deal of pain, and Shipman administered what was the standard painkiller for childbirth: pethidine.

How much of the drug had Shipman given Susan? The exact amount is unknown, but it was later speculated by the Orlinskis to have been a dangerously high amount. The pethidine would have not only affected Susan but the baby too. Little Christian was born with the opioid in his bloodstream and immediately had trouble breathing.

When things seemed under control, the family went home, but less than a day later, they noticed Christian was turning blue. The situation only grew more dire by the time Shipman arrived, and the new parents expected the doctor to call an ambulance. Shipman did not do this despite the urgency, and the baby soon died.

"We were young and naïve and trusted Shipman," Mark Orlinski would later regretfully recall. "We were frantic and didn't know what to do. In the chaos and confusion, we basically let him get away with it. But we knew it was his fault."

Was little Christian murdered? Probably not. It appears that the infant's untimely death was more a consequence of Shipman's insistence on doing things his way than any actual malice. This is evidenced by the profound effect the death had on Shipman. Friends would say that the ordeal was incredibly upsetting, almost traumatic, for the doctor.

In any case, Shipman would only become more unhinged following this incident. He'd already had problems with drugs by the time he left Pontefract, but now his ability to hide it was worsening – as was his fascination with death. He began to do strange things in order to satisfy his curiosity.

One unfortunate guinea pig of Shipman's interests was twenty-five-year-old clerk Elaine Oswald. While she was in overall good health, she had recently been experiencing an unusual pain in her side that she worried could be appendicitis. She was shocked when she went to see Dr. Shipman, and he told her instead that she was suffering from a severe case of kidney stones.

Like the Orlinskis, Oswald trusted the doctor entirely. She thought nothing of it when he prescribed her opioids and told her that he would need to make a house call later to draw her blood. She was unaware that a blood test was unnecessary; had Shipman truly believed she could have a kidney stone, he would have requested a sample of her urine. Oswald did as she was told but decided to wait until later to fill out the prescription and take the medication. It was a decision that likely saved her life.

By the time Shipman was at her bedside, she could hardly keep her eyes open. He spoke to her, but she did not register what he was saying. She could remember the feeling of him drawing her blood, but then he did the unexpected: he injected her with something. But she would not have time to question his actions; before long, the young woman was out cold.

For a short while, Oswald remained unconscious. When she began to stir, she realized that Shipman was still there, along with his wife and toddler-aged son. An ambulance crew was also there – but why?

Suddenly, Shipman slapped her across the face. Oswald was startled awake for a moment but started drifting off again as the crew placed her into the ambulance. Shipman accompanied her for the ride, slapping her hard whenever he thought she was losing consciousness again.

When she arrived at the hospital, she was covered in bruises, and her mouth was cut. She explained to the staff that she had only taken the exact amount of medication she had been prescribed, two tablets of dipipanone. They would not believe her. Based on the severity of her reaction, they thought she had overdosed on something else, something possibly illegal.

Oswald spent four more days in that hospital, wondering what could possibly have happened to her. The ordeal had left her in poor condition, and she would need to spend around a month recovering at home. She was tended to by her husband, Peter, and every now and then, Shipman made house calls.

Unlike the suspicious hospital staff, Shipman appeared to express greater concern for her wellbeing. Most importantly for Oswald, he tried to get to the bottom of what happened to her that evening. He concluded that she must have had an allergic reaction to the dipipanone, and it was an explanation that she felt comfortable with.

Shipman's care did not end there. He wanted to keep in touch with her to ensure that her health was improving. He invited her and Peter to the new Shipman house for dinner. Like most people who met the woman, Oswald felt that Primrose was a little bit odd, very quiet, and a good cook.

"I got the impression that she adored her husband and thought that he hung the moon and the stars," Oswald would go on to say. "As did I at the time. He was my hero; he had just saved my life."

Her image of Shipman as her savior would remain intact until she heard of him getting arrested nearly three decades later for suspicion of murder. The drug he used on her, in addition to the dipipanone, which she would later find out she was not allergic to at all, was pethidine. Oswald would also state that she believed Shipman had drugged and attempted to kill her for his sexual gratification.

This was possible but unlikely. Given the events that would follow, it appears far more likely that Shipman was trying to test if the amount of pethidine he gave her could have potentially been lethal. This was not only for his potential future victims but for himself. He only focused on saving her when it was clear that his plans had been thwarted.

He was, in any case, already hoarding large amounts of the drug, some of which was clearly to feed his own addiction. He was filling out prescriptions for both the center's supply – at the time, Ormerod did not keep a proper register of their drugs – as well as for individual patients, many of whom did not even need it. The fact that he was heading down to the pharmacy to pick up the medications himself should have been enough to raise some eyebrows.

Other than the unfortunate death of Christian Orlinski, it does not appear that Shipman was responsible for more deaths in 1974. The following year, however, was a different story. It was as though some repressed urge had almost completely taken over him; not even a month into 1975, Shipman had already claimed three victims.

All three died on the same day, January 21st. The first victim was an elderly woman named Elizabeth Pierce. Shipman was believed to have been on a house call with her when she suddenly passed, but the fact that all possible witnesses had already died by the time the Inquiry was launched meant that her death was never officially ruled a murder. The next victim was sixty-three-year-old Bob Lingard. Lingard was already in poor health, and his family had been told by other medical professionals that he would soon die. This is likely why nobody questioned anything when Lingard died while Shipman was visiting.

Shockingly, Shipman would arrive at the home of his third victim just a few minutes after killing Bob Lingard. Lily Crossley, a terminal cancer patient, lived for only an hour following Shipman's visit.

More deaths followed in the coming months. In March, he began regularly tending to sixty-nine-year-old Eva Lyons. The woman, a retired mill worker, had esophageal cancer and was in constant pain. She had recently undergone radiation therapy and seemed to have been doing better, but the treatment caused her to lose her hair and left her weak. It was a comfort to her and her husband to have as good a doctor as Shipman at their side. Every two days, he would make a house call with Lyons and her husband, Dick. He had also given her an intravenous shunt to keep the supply of painkillers she took steady.

It was late in the evening when Mrs. Lyons died, and nothing appeared to be out of the ordinary. The couple seemed to have been in good spirits despite their circumstances; they chatted with Shipman as he prepared to give her his usual injection.

Dick knew something was wrong when Shipman went silent. "Oh," said the doctor a moment later. "She's dead." The casual way he announced it struck Mr. Lyons. He would later tell his daughter, Norma, that Shipman had said it "as if he was announcing a bingo number or football score."

That was the end of Shipman's visit. He made no effort to check Mrs. Lyons's pulse for any possible signs of life, nor did he try to resuscitate her or call for an ambulance. The only thing he did before he left was to offer some of the sedative painkillers he used on the woman to her husband in order to calm him down. Mr. Lyons, understandably reeling after having lost his wife so suddenly, declined the injection.

His time at Ormerod remained otherwise uneventful until, around the same time as Eva Lyons's murder, Shipman's dark secret slowly began to come to light.

The numerous prescriptions he had written for pethidine, as well as his own unusual habit of getting the drugs himself, had not gone unnoticed. He narrowly managed to avoid questioning when the Home Office Drug Inspectorate, as well as the West Yorkshire Police Drugs Squad, first paid a visit to the pharmacies he frequented. Shipman's good reputation preceded him, and the officers left assured that the prescriptions were entirely legitimate.

But concerns were raised again in May of 1975. Shipman had never been known to suffer from any major health problems, but he was suddenly experiencing random fainting spells, sometimes while at work in front of patients. One evening while at home, Shipman was in the bathroom when he blacked out and hit his head. Terrified, Primrose called her husband's partners at Ormerod, who helped get him to a nearby hospital.

He had suffered a concussion. After reaching out to a specialist, the diagnosis they gave him was epilepsy, but why Shipman was suddenly suffering from it now at this stage in life, and with seemingly no trigger, stumped the other doctors. None of them could have predicted what the true cause of these episodes would turn out to be.

Shipman, perhaps in an attempt to keep up appearances, decided to finally heed all the advice that came his way. Now considered an epileptic, he was no longer legally permitted to drive – he had been seen fainting in the parking lot. He gave up driving himself to work and instead had his wife take him to and from the center every day.

Suspicions arose as the mysterious blackouts continued. Little did his friends and peers know that the country's Home Office Drugs Inspectorate was hot on the doctor's trail again and had been since February 1975, months before the illness began. Law enforcement had taken notice of the fact that Shipman was still acquiring a substantial amount of pethidine and decided to interview the doctor himself.

Nowadays, pethidine, also commonly known as meperidine, is classified as a Class A controlled drug in the United Kingdom. This means that, while the drug still has its proper uses in a medical context such as childbirth, it can still be extremely dangerous if abused. However, the addictive properties of pethidine were not well understood in the early 1970s when it was first given that classification, and some medical experts even doubted that one could become addicted to the drug at all. It was considered to be a safer alternative to morphine and was widely used, with up to sixty percent of doctors surveyed in 1975 prescribing it to help manage pain. It has been revealed to be toxic over prolonged use.

While pethidine is still used today, attempts to hoard the drug as Shipman did would ring alarm bells long before it could become an issue.

The investigators who dropped the matter so easily before were now determined to get to the bottom of things. During the interview, Shipman appeared less like the genial, responsible doctor the pharmacists had described him as and presented himself as more ornery, almost mean. He vehemently denied that he was using the drug for personal use.

Still, not everyone was satisfied. Another investigation began in June when a particular supplier of pethidine noticed the unusual amount of prescriptions Shipman was submitting. This time, law enforcement conducted a search of the center, but they came away with little useful information. They did, however, meet with the other partners and fill them in on why they were investigating. The doctors, once so glad to have Shipman working alongside them, were stunned and outraged.

Shipman, who was used to keeping meticulous patient records, intentionally kept very little documentation of his practice's pethidine use. Keeping a record of how many times he administered the drug to patients was mandatory by law, but police could hardly prove that Shipman even had it in the first place.

Unfortunately for Shipman, the other doctors at the center were far less forgiving. Shipman might have been a good doctor on his own but having a drug-abusing partner in their practice would have reflected poorly on all of them. After the investigation that summer, the other partners, led by Dr. John Dacre, gathered evidence of Shipman's secret addiction – a simple discussion with the patients supposedly receiving pethidine revealed that many of them had not even known they had been prescribed it – and confronted him that September during a meeting.

The confrontation must have come as a shock to the doctor since his arrogance typically led him to believe that he was always one step ahead of everyone else. When he realized that he had failed to fool them all, he decided to use manipulation tactics.

Shipman admitted to his crime and secret shame in front of the other doctors, trying to appear noble. How could such a good doctor be struggling with something like this? He leaned in hard to this particular point: despite his substance abuse, he was still a much-loved and competent doctor. Why should they let his addiction to a seemingly harmless drug get in the way of his work? If anything, pethidine might have even made him better at his job.

They were not just his peers but also his friends, were they not? Shipman argued that if they cared about him, their patients, and their community, the best thing to do would be to sweep the entire matter under the rug. That, and they could help him get hold of more pethidine to keep the facade going.

55

Unsurprisingly, the other partners soundly rejected this outlandish idea. They told him that he needed to seek treatment, and in the meantime, he would be replaced. Shipman then went home, ostensibly in agreement with his partners.

It was, of course, just an act. This rejection brought his inner darkness out. Shipman became enraged and returned to the center hours later. His aloof, composed demeanor turned sour as he insulted and cursed at the other men. He tore his stethoscope from his coat and threw it on the ground, insisting that they would never get him to leave. If they wanted him gone, he said, they would have to force him out.

A short while later, Primrose would make an appearance at the center herself. She was now twenty-six and had become more devoted – some might say borderline fanatical – to her husband in their nine years together. She raged at her husband's partners, repeating his insistence that he was not going anywhere without a fight.

In reality, there was little the couple could do when the doctors did make the decision to kick Shipman out of the practice. Together, they had gathered enough evidence of Shipman's drug habits to get him investigated yet again, this time in late

November. By then, he had already checked into a drug rehabilitation center and was more or less expecting the police to come knocking.

This time, Shipman made no effort to deny the accusations, though it is unclear if this was another attempt to manipulate investigators or if the doctor had finally found himself backed into a corner. He readily admitted that he had a problem and that he had developed this habit to cope with stress – the death of Christian Orlinski came to mind. Being a doctor was no easy job, he emphasized, especially when he had such a hard time getting along with the other partners.

Shipman's former partners would only hear about his claims sometime later after the matter had been mostly wrapped up and written about in the local papers. It came as a genuine surprise to them to read about how Shipman had supposedly developed depression due to their inability to get along with him. If anything, it was Shipman himself who had a hard time playing nice.

Of course, this had all been a ploy by Shipman to begin with. During the investigation, a detective found that all of Shipman's veins had collapsed. This was the result of several years' worth of drug abuse, not the mere months that he claimed. For things to have gotten this bad, it meant that Shipman had been using pethidine right out of medical school.

Despite this damning evidence, the police decided not to look into this further.

As for Shipman's patients in Todmorden, gossip spread quickly among them. While his reputation in the area was forever tarnished, not everyone was so hard on the disgraced doctor.

"There was sympathy for him," recalled one former patient. "There was an attitude of, poor bugger, he's worked too hard, and it's all become too much for him."

Reluctantly, Shipman finally sought treatment. He was soon admitted to a renowned private psychiatric center in York known as The Retreat. After a week-long detox period, he was diagnosed with moderate depression and prescribed antidepressants. The new medication seemed to help his attitude greatly. Before long, he was discharged into an uncertain future.

V

Getting Off Easy

SHORTLY AFTER CHRISTMAS 1976, HAROLD Shipman was discharged from the drug rehabilitation center where he had been receiving treatment for his pethidine addiction. Upon his release, he claimed to be a changed man. Not only had he graciously accepted the recommendation to receive psychiatric supervision for the foreseeable future, but he had also made a promise to never again take up employment at any practice where he might have access to pethidine.

Life behind the scenes was not so positive. The loss of his job meant that he could no longer keep up with the mortgage on their house, and as a result, Primrose and their two children moved in with her parents. Their house in Todmorden was successfully sold, but it almost did not happen.

During all the time they had been together, Primrose had been known for being a terrific housewife. Thanks to the training and old-fashioned values her mother had worked so hard to instill, she was a good cook, planning elaborate meals for whenever her husband brought over guests, though she always made herself scarce when company came. The homes they lived in, while not spotless, were well-maintained.

Somewhere along the way, everything fell apart for Primrose.

Never particularly extroverted, she had become reclusive in recent months. Neighbors considered her to be loud-mouthed and bossy. The other doctors' wives at Ormerod disliked her because they thought she was petty. The Shipman's younger child, Christopher, was said to walk around in dirty clothes, his diaper full.

But none of that compared to the state of the Shipman home. When a potential buyer came to see the property, she was disgusted to see how filthy it was. Trash and other clutter overflowed through almost every room. It was so bad that she needed to assemble a team of friends to help remove everything before she closed on the deal.

What happened to Primrose Shipman? Had she given up? Had the stress of raising two young children with a workaholic-turned-drug-addict husband finally gotten to her? One might note that the more devoted to her husband she became, the lower she seemed to sink.

We do not know if Shipman was ever abusive to his wife – his children, understandably, avoid the spotlight and do not give interviews. Those who knew the couple recall that the doctor had a tendency to "remind" his wife that he was the smarter one in the relationship, the breadwinner, the one in control of their lives. Before him, there were her parents. Primrose never held the reigns of her own life.

Primrose's decline had all the signs of someone suffering deeply, but we can only speculate as to the cause.

As for Shipman himself, things were actually looking up again for the disgraced doctor. Now that he was off pethidine, his mysterious seizures stopped about as suddenly as they began. His improved health meant he was able to drive himself around again, getting back his independence. But perhaps what he was most pleased with was how lightly he was getting off for his crimes.

In February, he was brought to the Halifax Magistrates' Court, where he faced three charges of obtaining pethidine by deception, three charges of illegal possession of pethidine, and one charge of prescription forgery – he had forged the signature of the head of a nursing home. Shipman decided it was best not to try and defend himself again and pleaded guilty to all charges.

This would turn out to work in his favor. Shockingly, despite being convicted on every charge, the doctor would face no jail time. Instead, he had to pay up. For every charge, he was to pay a fee of seventy-five pounds. In total, he would end up paying six hundred pounds, around fifty-three hundred pounds in today's currency – around sixty-four hundred American dollars. The court allowed him to pay in increments of fifty pounds a month.

It was a lot of money for an unemployed father of two to pay. Once again, help came from the Oxtobys. Despite their chilly relationship with Shipman and their daughter, the older couple adored their two grandchildren. Unfortunately for Primrose, their assistance was yet another thing her parents would hold over her head, no doubt worsening the already tense relationship.

Relief came soon for the younger couple, and Shipman went on to have little trouble paying the sum himself, as he had already acquired a new job earlier that same month. On February 2nd, he was hired as a clinical medical officer at the Newton Aycliffe Health Centre. There, he would work primarily with children. It certainly helped that this new job, located in Durham, was over a hundred miles away from his past life.

Since this position did not initially grant Shipman access to controlled substances, his new employers had no issue hiring him despite having been informed of his addiction and related crimes. They were further reassured by his psychiatrists, who were still treating him.

Shipman adjusted well to this new job, so much so that his employers were willing to stick up for him after his convictions were brought to the attention of the General Medical Council – an organization that registers medical practitioners in the United Kingdom. When a GMC member faced criminal charges, their case was often brought before the Penal Cases Committee. This meant that a member who did not face jail time, such as Shipman, could still be disciplined in some other way by the groups invested in keeping doctors from misconduct. Luckily for him, his employers wrote a glowing letter of support that showed he was likely not in danger of relapsing.

This, along with input from his psychiatrists, helped Shipman come away with little more than a warning. Though Shipman had sworn to never work a position that would give him access to the kind of drugs he had been abusing, he readily reneged on his word as soon as the opportunity presented itself. The court decided that as he had learned his lesson, successfully sought treatment, and did not sell pethidine or deny it to patients who truly needed it, there would be no harm in letting him have access to controlled substances once again.

Shipman's lack of consequences was likely due to his positive reputation. Though he might have been difficult to work with, according to the other doctors, his actual patients could not seem to say enough good things about him. Additionally, he had only used the drugs on himself and never used pethidine irresponsibly on those under his care. At least, not that anyone knew of at the time. His preferred drug for murder was diamorphine. This, coupled with the fact that this was Shipman's first and only major crime, meant that he was free to continue his work practically unsupervised.

The whole ordeal must have shaken Shipman to his core. He had come close to not only never being allowed access to his precious pethidine again but also never being allowed to work as a doctor in any capacity. They had been merciful to him this time, but he could not risk getting caught again.

That mercy was a grave error on the Committee's part – one that would prove to have casualties in the hundreds. Shipman may have gotten himself "clean" from the pethidine, but in all other ways, he refused to change. The only lesson he truly learned was how to hide better.

VI

The Private Practice

SHIPMAN WOULD ONLY BE AT THE NEWTON Aycliffe Health Centre for a short time. Within a few months, in 1977, he was already looking for a new job now that he was free of all legal restraints. His search brought him to the Donneybrook Medical Centre, a practice in the town of Hyde in the Greater Manchester area that needed a general practitioner.

Once again, he was up front about his past issues, even allowing his new employers to speak with his past psychiatrists, who all said Shipman was in good mental shape. His potential new partners were impressed by his honesty and were happy to have him join their ranks, which he did officially in October 1977.

Much like his early days at Ormerod, Shipman's inclusion on the medical team came as a relief to his employers. He was only thirty-one years old and still young enough for his medical school knowledge to be considered the most up-to-date among his peers. In particular, he was an expert in record-keeping. Later, he would become known for advocating for regular patient check-ups to prevent illness. These skills would allow him to stay at Donneybrook for the next several years.

Hyde was a quiet, largely unassuming place. At the time, its population was comprised of honest, working-class families, some of which had fallen on hard times but maintained a strong sense of community. Long-time residents, however, could recall a grim history in its not-too-distant past. In the summers, the foul stench that emanated from the Smith Brothers animal by-products factory would grow so bad that people were forced to change their ways of life to better endure it. Things like keeping all the windows of their homes shut during heatwaves and the schools tracking weather patterns to gauge the odor were commonplace.

The closure of the factory should have come as a relief to the residents of Hyde – if only it had not left so many without a job.

But a bad smell was little compared to the town's other claim of infamy. The name Hyde may already be familiar to some true crime readers. It was not far from here where, in the 1960s, serial killer duo Ian Brady and Myra Hindley, also known as the Moors Murderers, killed a ten-year-old girl and seventeen-year-old boy. These heinous crimes were still fresh in the residents' memories when another murderer would draw attention back to the area: Dr. Harold Shipman.

In the meantime, Shipman was busy once again becoming a pillar of the local community. He was the young, sharp but caring doctor who all the patients preferred. He was known for spending his lunch periods doing house calls. When he was not having lengthy and thorough check-ups with the patients at Donneybrook, he was dividing his time between being a volunteer surgeon for the St. John Ambulance – an organization that provides and teaches first aid – and doing secretarial work for the Tameside Local Medical Committee.

Dr. Ian Naper, who was also employed at the practice, held a high opinion of the new partner:

"He was well liked by patients because he would put himself out for them. He would volunteer to visit them," explained Naper. "Most doctors see a patient and say to them 'If it's not better in a day or two, give us a ring.' Fred would say, 'I'll drop by in a couple of days to see how you're doing.' It made a very heavy workload, but he didn't seem to mind. He was everybody's idea of an old-fashioned doctor."

He was also making good money. Donneybrook had seven doctors, including Shipman, in one large facility. While they all shared staff such as nurses, receptionists, and assistants, each doctor kept their own list of patients. The longer the list, the more money they could potentially earn. Shipman's popularity meant that he had a list over two thousand names long.

The recovery of the family's finances meant that Shipman could once again afford a mortgage, albeit in a less than spectacular house. The house was large enough for the family – they would have two more children in the coming years – but it was said to look shabby. Shipman, always keen to do things his own way, was said to have added to the house despite having no knowledge of building construction. The house would only grow shabbier the deeper he sank into his depravity.

As time went on, Shipman would also begin to reveal his true, darker self.

It began, as it had before, with his attitude. He grew older, and his methods of doing things gradually became outdated. Medical technology continued to advance, and he was no longer the expert he had once been. Shipman would always struggle to accept the possibility that he was not as superior to others as he believed. He took out these frustrations on those unlucky enough to work beside him.

One particularly memorable incident happened after Shipman had settled in. A young drug representative arrived early that morning and sat in the lobby, waiting anxiously for the doctors to have some free time. It was her first day on the job, and she felt intimidated like most people would in her shoes.

The job was not an easy one. Being a drug representative meant spending lots of time on the road, going to medical practice after medical practice, and pitching the company's newest medications to doctors far more experienced in health than she was, all to convince them to carry the product. Although it was a daunting task trying to sell something to experts, everything seemed fine to the representative so far.

Out of Donneybrook's seven doctors, only three or four of them could meet with her that day. In a way, she thought, that made things easier. Upstairs, the small group of doctors huddled around the table in a meeting room while she prepared her pitch.

The representative knew that doctors were often less than enthusiastic about sitting through these meetings but thankfully, everyone had been polite so far. This gave her some courage, and she finally began her presentation. She was going over the benefits of this new medication and its advantages over its competitors when she noticed that one of the doctors had stopped smiling.

His look became one of scorn, then rage. The representative soldiered on until he suddenly got up from his chair and began to pace around the small room. She had just opened her mouth to try and speak again when he rushed to close the gap between them, putting his bespectacled face alarmingly close to hers.

"Asking questions" is perhaps too gentle of a term for what the doctor did next. He interrogated her like a criminal, demanding to know how someone like her could possibly know the real benefits of a new medication. Stunned, the woman tried helplessly to keep up with his questions, but he berated her before she could even open her mouth.

"You don't even know the side-effect profile of this drug you expect us to use on our patients!" he barked.

The cruel doctor's composure continued to deteriorate even further. He was a belligerent mess, screaming incoherently at the woman. When he, at last, had enough, he lumbered out of the room, slamming the door shut behind him.

His partners were in disbelief. The representative, who had been so anxious for the meeting, stood frozen before them. She could not help but cry; all the yelling had shaken her up badly.

Luckily, the other doctors were gracious enough to comfort her, offering her tea and expressing that they had never known Shipman to behave like this before. He had always been so polite. It was a sign of worse things to come.

While he continued to put on a friendly face for the patients, his partners and other staff were often exposed to this crueler side. His insults grew more frequent as his own methods grew outdated. He simply could not accept that his methods were not the best and was angered whenever someone tried to do something different. Shipman, it was determined, simply did not play well with others, and having to abide by the rules and practices of the other partners was stifling to him.

"He was known for his bad temper," said Vivian Langfield, the former manager of the practice. "It was a joke among reception staff. We would tease each other: 'If you do that again, you'll have Fred blowing his top!' We would say good morning to the doctors as they arrived, but Fred would never reply. He would just go to his office, the last one at the end of the corridor, without saying a word. He never responded to our greetings. We all felt that he was ignorant."

Shipman saw himself as the intellectual superior to nurses, cleaners, and receptionists, paying them little attention unless they did something to annoy him. New employees, however, he would welcome and treat warmly, especially those who expressed admiration for him – until, of course, they did anything he disagreed with.

"I am a good doctor!" Shipman would snap. "I have all the qualifications from Leeds Medical School! I have passed all my exams!"

Shipman was a menace to Langfield. Though she was not a low-ranking member of the staff, Shipman still considered himself to be better than her. He criticized her constantly, telling her that she was too inept for the job and ought to quit or demanded that she fire whichever hapless worker had annoyed him that day. When she refused to give in, he stopped speaking to her entirely, instead insisting that she leave him notes on his desk.

Langfield believed that the other partners were somewhat afraid of Shipman. They rarely intervened and usually cowered to his demands. Gradually, they distanced themselves from him, as well as Primrose, who the doctors' wives saw as cold and strange. Indeed, the couple was becoming reclusive again; Shipman abruptly withdrew from all his charity work, and Primrose let the house become filthy again.

In 1985, Shipman's father died suddenly after a heart attack. Those around him at the practice tried to express that they were sorry to hear about his loss. "Are you?" Shipman snapped in reply. "I'm not." By now, both he and Primrose had effectively cut off both of their families.

Shipman, of course, had seen a lot of death in his time. Is it possible that he had become desensitized to the loss of human life? By August 1978, he had begun killing again. His first victim was Sarah Hannah Marsland – an eighty-six-year-old woman whose daughter, Irene Chapman, would also later die at his hands. Later that same month, he murdered Mary Ellen Jordan, who was seventy-three. In December, he murdered Harold Bramwell, seventy-three, and Annie Campbell, eighty-eight. He slowed down in 1979 and waited until that August to kill Alice Maude Gorton, seventy-six. His next victim was a seventy-seven-year-old man whose death nearly required a post-mortem examination. This was entirely unexpected and no doubt caused Shipman some fear. Once that worry had passed, Shipman would restrain his urges until 1981, when he again killed two women in their eighties while making his usual house calls in Hyde.

For whatever reason, Shipman did not kill again until 1983. Again, two people. His killing increased by a large margin by the end of the decade. He would have fifty-seven murders during this time. A curious number of them happened around the holidays, and there were sometimes up to four victims a week. By 1989, he had become bold enough to murder a woman, eighty-one-year-old Mary Hamer, right there at the practice instead of in her home.

Mrs. Hamer's death puzzled the other doctors. Despite her age, she was an active woman in good health and high spirits. She had come in one day for a usual check-up when she supposedly suffered a heart attack. Shipman claimed to have given her an injection for her pain and left her alone for just a moment to call the ambulance and, during that moment, Mrs. Hamer died.

There was never any evidence of this call for an ambulance, and it was likely all a lie.

It was hardly a surprise then when in 1991, after fourteen years at Donneybrook, Shipman announced his plans to leave the practice to work independently. When questioned as to why, he explained that he was dissatisfied with the new computer system they were using – no doubt it was one he had not been able to master – and he disapproved of the way Donneybrook handled their government-allocated funds. He left the practice with over seventy victims under his belt.

He had so many victims that, by the 90s, it had reached a point where the majority of them are largely not referred to by name in most sources. Countless victims got lost in the list of those he murdered or was suspected of murdering, becoming little more than a number or notch on the scoreboard of a demented killer.

By early 1992, he had opened his own private practice at 21 Market Street in Hyde, a town in Manchester. Once again, his good reputation preceded him; many patients and even some lower-end staff members came with him to his new office. While this was a source of financial woes for his old partners, it was welcome work for Shipman, who was now raising four children with his wife.

Much to the chagrin of the Donneybrook doctors, Shipman's private practice would prove to be extremely popular. His patients considered him to be such a good doctor that they eagerly recommended him to friends and family. Before long, his patient list grew so long that getting accepted as a new patient was likened to having won the lottery.

All the while, he was doing the unthinkable to those who came to him for help.

VII

The Best Doctor in Hyde

HAROLD SHIPMAN WAS CONSIDERED BY MORE than a few people to be the best doctor in Hyde. Shipman's warm demeanor was a welcome change for the elderly and chronically ill, who were often well-acquainted with the typical discomfort of medical appointments. In fact, he was known for going above and beyond for his patients.

If they needed an expensive drug, Shipman would get it for them. "This is going to cost me a hundred pounds," he would reassure them. "But it's what you need, so you shall have it." If a patient needed a sling, Shipman would make one for them by hand until they could get another. Nervous or depressed patients often found themselves smiling in his presence. He was quick with a joke, confident in his words, and remembered little details about their lives. It was a blessing for those whose age and ill health often left them socially isolated.

He was not just popular with elderly patients, either. "I had gone to him a couple of times for emergency contraception," recalled former patient Rebecca Evans. "The morning-after pill, and he prescribed it without question. He was never judgmental. Young people could go to him with any problems. You could talk to him about drugs, pregnancy, anything that was bothering you... He said, 'If it bothers you enough to come see me, it's not stupid.'"

Where Shipman truly shined was when it came to making house calls.

Nowadays, the thought of doctors making house calls may seem like something more from the turn of the century than the 1990s, especially for those of us outside of the United Kingdom. In reality, house calls remained a cornerstone of UK medicine until around 2019, when the National Health Service voted to put a stop to them, citing resource and scheduling restraints. Had Harold Shipman stayed in medicine, he almost certainly would have continued to make regular visits to patient homes for as long as he was able to.

After all, the privacy that came with house calls made it easy to kill.

He had grown smarter about covering his tracks. Certain drugs, such as potent opioids like morphine, can stay in the tissues of the human body long after death, especially when administered in just a few massive doses. For this reason, Shipman often suggested cremation to the families of his deceased patients, effectively burning up the evidence against him.

Creating a solid timeline of Shipman's murders is practically impossible for this reason. Not only for the loss of evidence in possible cremated victims but also for the sheer number of them.

Harold Shipman is believed to be the most prolific serial killer not only in the United Kingdom but in all of modern history, and this is by a considerable margin. In total, he is known to have had at least two hundred eighteen victims, though some estimates are two hundred fifty to five hundred victims. For reference, the second most prolific serial killer is believed to be

Luis Garavito from Colombia, with one hundred ninety-three victims.

To kill so many people, murder must have been a constant activity, something like a second job to Shipman. He was known to be meticulous, even obsessive, when it came to patient records. Given how long he worked in medicine, as well as how early into his career he might have started killing, it is easy to see how the search for a final death toll continues to climb even now.

So, it remains a tragic fact that the majority of Shipman's two hundred eighteen canonical victims are seldom thought of as anything more than ticks on the scorecard of a deranged doctor. Though The Shipman Inquiry made much of the information surrounding Shipman's crimes available to the public, the lives of so many people are understandably reduced to a list of names and a collection of witness statements. To list them all in this book, unfortunately, would not be possible, but the effort to tell as much of their stories as possible should still be made.

What we do know is that his first victim at The Surgery was eighty-two-year-old Joan Harding. Like Mary Hamer, Harding was a healthy woman with no major medical issues. She complained of a slight ache in her shoulder and went to see Dr.

Shipman for it while a friend waited for her in the parking lot. Shipman injected her under the guise of drawing her blood. Then, Harding died, supposedly of a heart attack.

The pain in her shoulder likely made his story more believable, as many people experience pain in their arm before suffering a heart attack, though this is more common in men than women.

Then there was sixty-eight-year-old Bertha Moss. After her was eighty-seven-year-old Dora Ashton, followed by seventy-two-year-old Edith Brady. All of these women were in decent health when they died unexpectedly at Shipman's practice.

For as patient and hard-working as Shipman seemed on the outside, he was still an easy person to annoy. In 1997, he had grown tired of sixty-three-year-old Ivy Lomas, who he claimed was a hypochondriac. She came by for real and imagined health problems so frequently that Shipman joked that the practice ought to have saved a special seat for her in the waiting room.

He was especially cold when Lomas died. Shipman gave the usual injection and then left her alone in the room. He went on treating other patients while Lomas began slipping away. It would be a while before he let his staff know that the woman had died, and he made no effort to resuscitate her even after police expected it.

Meanwhile, Shipman's attitude and behavior continued to grow stranger.

When one pictures a medical office or hospital, one likely expects little by way of decoration. There may be some posters or charts on the waiting room wall and a few paintings in the hallways. After all, these places are meant to be tidy and efficient. But in the 1990s, the untidiness of the Shipman home had seemingly begun to spread to the practice, and Shipman's preference for décor was pigs.

The Surgery had pigs everywhere. There were pig paintings and ornaments in every room. He even kept a large piggy bank in the front office for collecting donations.

His odd behavior was noticed by his former partners. Doctors in the United Kingdom, particularly general practitioners like Shipman, are expected to continue to attend advanced medical lectures at local universities to keep their knowledge up-to-date. As far as Shipman was concerned, however, he already knew everything he needed. Much to the embarrassment of his peers, he would hardly let the lecturer start before he began berating them about their qualifications.

The number of deaths he certified was numerous; the fact stands that, in the end, Shipman was only ever convicted of the murder of fifteen women who died within a span of three years, from 1995 to 1998.

It was also in 1998 that people finally began publicly voicing their suspicions of Hyde's favorite doctor. Ironically, it was Shipman's constant insistence on cremation that raised eyebrows among other local doctors.

In the United Kingdom, multiple forms must be signed and reviewed before the deceased person can be cremated. The first form, Form B, is filled out by the doctor who had been tending to the patient before their passing. This means that the process was always started out by and handled, in part, by Shipman. It required him to fill out information such as their time of death as well as the cause, which he had a habit of either exaggerating or outright fabricating.

The next step in this process was also prime for corruption. A second doctor unaffiliated with the first, such as one employed at another medical practice, would review Form B as well as the body of the deceased. This was to ensure that there was nothing suspicious at hand, but the fact that the second doctor could get paid for their part meant that some were more willing to overlook anything unusual.

The third and final step was Form F. This was signed by medical professionals, often at the crematorium itself. By the time all the information was passed down to them, they had already received the "okay" from two separate doctors, which meant that they were not likely looking at everything with as much of a keen eye as they could have.

Then, the body was cremated, and any evidence still in the body went up in flames.

Though the Form C step could be abused through money, it was actually at this step where Dr. Linda Reynolds, a partner at the Brooke Surgery, noticed something was off. Shipman was limited to making Form C requests to doctors within a certain vicinity. The fact that the Brooke Surgery was located directly across the street from Shipman's own practice meant that they most often went there. The staggering number of Form C requests puzzled Dr. Reynolds.

To put that amount in perspective, the Brooke Surgery, which had multiple doctors and a patient list almost three times the size of Shipman's, had fewer patient deaths happen within three months than Shipman had at sixteen deaths. To make things worse, those Form C deaths realistically only accounted for a small portion of patient deaths at Shipman's hands, as some requests were sent elsewhere, and some patients were not cremated at all.

The suspicions were not limited to the cremated victims, either. Around the same time Dr. Reynolds raised the alarm, a local undertaker had noticed a number of strange similarities when it came to his deceased patients. Funeral director Alan Massey, who was often tasked with collecting the bodies, could not help but wonder why so many of the deceased were found seated, fully clothed, as though they had been simply going through the motions of their daily lives when they dropped dead without warning.

When Massey brought his concerns to Shipman, the doctor reassured him by providing extensive medical records. Indeed, the circumstances of their deaths, odd as they were, always matched up to the information Shipman kept on file.

Though not entirely reassured, Massey dropped the issue. After all, he had no way of knowing that Shipman had a habit of going back and rewriting patient records to match the stories he fed their families.

But not everyone was convinced. The skeptics included Debbie Brambroffe, Massey's daughter and a funeral director in her own right. After sharing her suspicions with Dr. Reynolds and other local doctors who received Form C requests, they reported their findings to law enforcement.

Sadly, the first police investigation into Shipman's activities at Hyde was botched from the start. No effort was made to look into Shipman's criminal past when a history of drug hoarding and prescription forgery would have otherwise brought up red flags. Once again, Shipman was able to deceive his doubters through his falsified records, and the investigation all but came to an end.

It would not be long, however, until Shipman's own arrogance would finally bring the end to a career of killing.

VIII

Mrs. Grundy

ON THE SURFACE, KATHLEEN GRUNDY WAS JUST like the rest of Shipman's victims: elderly, female, and widowed. She was eighty-one years old, had lost her husband John back in the 1960s, and was a regular patient at Shipman's practice. Another similarity between her and the countless others was the fact that Grundy adored Shipman and had followed him from Donneybrook when he decided to go private. Reportedly, she had even given a sizeable donation to his patients' fund.

Where Kathleen Grundy differed was in the fact that she was an incredibly popular woman. She had many friends who always spoke highly of her and, after her death, would reminisce about her seemingly endless generosity. Though she did not work, she spent much of her time volunteering and had even served as Hyde's mayor in the past.

It was her fellow volunteers who first noticed her missing. On Wednesday, June 24, 1998, she had been expected to arrive at the Werneth House, which functioned as something of a community center, after a routine doctor's appointment. The others were deep into preparing lunches when someone brought up how uncharacteristic it was of her to be late.

That comment got everyone's attention. Then, when Mrs. Grundy failed to show up entirely, they knew something had to be wrong. If being late was unusual for her, canceling on them without a word was unimaginable given how organized the woman always was. When numerous phone calls to her house went unanswered, John Green, a nursing home caretaker, and Ronald Pickford, another volunteer and friend, took it upon themselves to check up on Mrs. Grundy in person.

There was no need to knock. Strangely, her front door had been left unlocked, so the men carefully entered, calling out for their friend. They soon found her lying on the living room sofa.

At first, they assumed Mrs. Grundy had only been sleeping. She was still in her day clothes and had curled up as though she had decided to take an impromptu nap. It was only when they got closer that they realized her face had turned ghostly pale.

Mrs. Grundy was dead. Nobody saw it coming.

Shipman, as her doctor, was one of the first people to be contacted after the discovery. He confirmed that he had seen her earlier that day, and she had complained about sudden chest pains she had never experienced before.

Word of these pains got back to Mrs. Grundy's only daughter, Angela Woodruff. Mrs. Woodruff was not only stunned by her mother's death but also confused as to how it happened. Her mother had been an active and fit woman, regularly going on long walks a few times a week. She only ever seemed to have suffered from a few minor medical issues that came with advanced age. There was also the fact that the two women communicated frequently, and Mrs. Grundy had never mentioned any chest pains.

In fact, Mrs. Grundy had been in such good shape that news of her passing baffled her many friends. "Did she get knocked over?" one of them reportedly asked. "I'd seen her jumping off a bus before it reached the stop a couple of weeks earlier, and the only way I could envisage her dying was in an accident. It was hard to believe she had died at home."

The post-mortem examination listed her official cause of death as simply "old age." This alone could have been enough to arouse suspicion, as "old age" is a rather nebulous term. It is almost always used in addition to an actual condition, such as a heart attack or stroke, and is hardly ever referred to as the cause of death itself.

Mrs. Grundy was laid to rest in the cemetery behind Hyde Chapel. Her headstone bore the words: "Died Unexpectedly After a Lifetime of Helping Others."

Mrs. Woodruff was only a few days into grieving when she got even more upsetting news. Her mother's will had changed – and drastically, at that. The cover letter read:

Dear Sir,

I enclose a copy of my will. I think it is clear in intent. I wish Dr. Shipman to benefit by having my estate but if he dies or cannot accept it, then the estate goes to my daughter.

I would like you to be the executor of my will. I intend to make an appointment to discuss this and my will in the near future.

Yours sincerely,

K. Grundy

This new will, which had been drafted and signed on June 9, 1998, was supposedly witnessed by someone who signed their name as "S. Smith" or "J. Smith." Mrs. Woodruff managed to track down this witness, who turned out to have been two people, a pet store owner and a young mother who were also patients of Shipman.

The pet store owner, identified later as a man named Paul Spencer, explained to Mrs. Grundy's daughter that he and the mother had been the only two people in the practice's waiting room that day when he asked them to come and witness a document signing. Reportedly, Spencer had been a little wary of the whole thing but quickly relented because of how much he trusted Dr. Shipman, who he likened to being like a "favorite uncle."

Mrs. Woodruff could not accept that her mother had suddenly, on her own, decided to leave absolutely nothing to her two beloved grandsons, Richard and Matthew. She would know what her mother really wanted more than anyone because she had always been the one in charge of her legal affairs. This included earlier drafts of her will, which she had kept in her office since the 1980s.

Even if Mrs. Woodruff had not been so thoroughly involved with her mother's will, odds are she would have suspected something was amiss. The will was both worded and typed rather poorly, and even the signature was off. It was far too large, and Mrs. Woodruff had more than enough samples of the real thing to prove that it looked nothing like Mrs. Grundy's handwriting.

Had Shipman known that the daughter of his latest victim was a keen-eyed practicing attorney, he might have avoided meddling with her will. Considering that Shipman was so popular in part because he liked to chat about his patients' personal lives and was known to memorize details about them, it seems unusual that he would overlook the profession of the only child of this notable patient.

Was it arrogance? Or had Shipman finally had enough of a career of killing over twenty years and decided it was time to get caught?

IX

A New Investigation

IT HAD BEEN A MISERABLE, RAINY NIGHT WHEN they exhumed Kathleen Grundy. The experience was a new one for the local police, as not even those among them with decades on the job had ever participated in digging up a body like this. Mrs. Grundy would actually prove to be the first person ever exhumed in the Greater Manchester area – and she would certainly not be the last.

The process left police feeling unsettled. Lack of experience meant they did not know that exhumations are typically carried out in the dark. This is to make sure there are as few people around as possible and spare the deceased's family members the trauma of seeing their loved one's coffin dug up.

Staff at a nearby nursing home were not informed of what was going on. Worried, the matron called the police only to be told that the cops were already at the scene and they were busy.

Thanks to Mrs. Woodruff's efforts, an investigation into her mother's death had been launched after she contacted Bernard Postles, the Detective Chief Superintendent, in late July. It helped when police realized that Shipman had, during that same year, been suspected of murdering his own patients.

On August 1, 1998, police obtained a warrant to search both Shipman's practice and home. They found much sought-after medical records but also an old Brother brand typewriter that they determined to have been the one used to write the new will. The typewriter proved to be an invaluable find in the case against Shipman. Though he claimed that he had loaned the machine to Mrs. Grundy to write out her will, only his fingerprints were ever found on the document, despite his insistence that she often borrowed it.

Around the same time, tissue and hair samples from Mrs. Grundy were sent off to different laboratories for testing. Her heart was in as decent a shape as it could have been after a month underground, and the assertion that she died of a heart attack looked ever more dubious.

The entire investigation caught Shipman by surprise. This was done intentionally so that he would have no chance to hide or destroy evidence. Police first searched The Surgery on a Saturday after all the patients had gone home. Shipman was locking up and clearly shocked to see them. Still, he put on his usual genial façade – that was until he realized that there was increasing suspicion against him, and his truer, arrogant self took over.

But it was the search at his house where they found more damning evidence.

The state of the house horrified the police. Though it looked decent enough on the outside, the inside was so dirty that even the experienced team could hardly stand the sight of it. Every inch of the place seemed to be covered in trash – discarded paper, filthy clothing, and old, moldy food. There was grime caked onto the walls, meaning that they needed to put on rubber gloves and other protective gear to search the place.

They found some of what they were looking for. Patient records were stuffed in unusual places in the house, such as in a duffel bag in the garage. What they had not been expecting was all the jewelry. There were rings, brooches, and necklaces of various worth stashed throughout the place. The majority of it was also women's jewelry, but they did not belong to either Primrose or Sarah Shipman.

Shipman himself was struggling to appear calm. He explained that sometimes before they passed, patients who were fond of him would leave something for The Surgery in their wills. It was usually not much, just small sums of money or jewelry that was worth even less. It was the same argument he had tried to pull with Mrs. Grundy's estate.

He must have realized then that his lies were falling apart all around him. He had gone too far and messed with the wrong lady.

Soon, the toxicology report for Mrs. Grundy's post-mortem examination came back, and they were startling. As previously mentioned, morphine is one of the few drugs that can be found in human tissues for a long time after death. Though by now it had been over a month since her passing, the laboratories managed to find that Mrs. Grundy had been administered a dose of morphine so high that it likely killed her in less than three hours.

Shipman defended himself by saying that Mrs. Grundy had become a drug addict and regularly came to his office seeking medications she did not need. Since so many people knew Mrs. Grundy personally, they told investigators that she had never shown any signs of substance abuse and that it was completely beyond her character to even suggest such a thing.

Shipman might have been a respected member of the Hyde community, but the fact that he made such an audacious claim against one of the few people possibly more well-regarded than him was the catalyst that began his undoing. He was arrested on September 7th of the same year under suspicion of murder and forgery.

Though the list of people who died under Shipman's care was seemingly endless, the upcoming trial would only focus on fifteen that were considered especially suspicious. Six of the bodies were cremated, but nine could still be exhumed. New post-mortem examinations showed that the victims, all of whom were elderly women, had high traces of morphine in their bodies. Only one of these women had ever been prescribed morphine or any other opiate. Indeed, they had little in common aside from age, gender, and their connection to Shipman.

By February 1999, Shipman was facing fifteen murder charges.

X

Odds Stacked Against Him

EVEN WITH ALL THE SUSPICION BUZZING around, Shipman would remain free to continue his work until August 21, 1999. It was not until news of the investigation spread wider to the media that he cracked. The doctor, once so convinced of his superiority over others, fell apart when faced with the consequences of his crimes. He was said to have become belligerent, nearly incomprehensible, and refused to comment on any questions he was asked. The evidence was stacking up against him, and it was clear that his defense was facing an uphill battle.

News of the murder charges shook the Hyde community. Many people desperately wanted to believe that the beloved doctor had been framed and were devastated to discover that this was not the case. Meanwhile, his wife, Primrose, always his biggest defender, now became his most ardent supporter. She told anyone who would listen that her husband was an innocent man.

Primrose was not the only person with an almost fanatical devotion to Shipman. Letters of support came pouring in, all of them attesting to the doctor's exceptional character. Long-time patients who had come to know the family sent cards offering their sympathy. Even those who were suspected of having lost their own family members at Shipman's hands insisted that he was the perfect doctor, and they would keep going to him no matter what. Indeed, The Surgery was busy up until its final day.

Leading the investigation was Detective Superintendent Bernard Postles. He was joined by Chief Detective Inspector Mike Williams and two more detective inspectors, Stan "The Hammer" Egerton and Steve Fullalove. These men had the unenviable task of looking through patient records and deciding who among them had most likely been murdered. In order to get through it all, they devised the following system:

Was the body buried or cremated? Score one for buried. (Cremated victims were, of course, much more difficult to investigate given the lack of a body.)

Was the family concerned about the circumstances of the death? Score one for yes.

Were there any causes for police concern (e.g., a cause of death not consistent with medical records, property missing, etc.) Score one for yes.

Had the medical records been altered. Score one for yes.

Give an extra point to any case which has scored four, making it a top priority.

This was how police managed to narrow down on the fifteen victims whose murders Shipman would be charged with.

The trial began October 5, 1999. In a controversial move, the court decided to try him on every charge through this one trial. This was despite efforts by his defense team to get him separate trials, including one just for Mrs. Grundy's death.

The prosecution had a mountain of evidence to go on, including witness statements that have not been mentioned. It was well-known that Shipman made house calls, and some of his patients reportedly looked so forward to these visits that they dressed in their finest clothing to receive him. However, in at least two cases, those of Jean Lilley and Marie West, Shipman had been seen in his patients' homes right before their sudden deaths. Lilley's lifeless body had been found by a neighbor after Shipman left.

The case of Marie West can be used as an example of Shipman's boldness while committing his crimes. West was eighty-one years old in 1995. She had leg pain and difficulty breathing at times but overall was not considered to be in poor health. He had arrived at West's home while she had been entertaining a friend, Maria Hadfield. Hadfield decided to move to the adjacent room to give her friend and the doctor some privacy, and before long, Shipman came to tell her that West had suffered a stroke. He then left the scene just as Hadfield realized her friend had died.

Family members on the witness stand would recall how callous Shipman was when he broke the tragic news. The once-kind doctor would barely even check for a pulse before declaring that the patient was gone and would instead start talking to them about how there was no need for a post-mortem examination and that they should consider cremation instead of a burial. In Marie West's case, he had been particularly callous. Before he left, he had opened the woman's eye and told her friend, "See? There's no life here anymore."

In some cases, such as when the victims passed in their homes after a visit from him, Shipman would claim that he had called an ambulance, only to cancel as soon as he saw there was no more need. Phone records revealed that no such calls had ever taken place. It was a lie Shipman committed time and time again.

The causes of death he listed for various women were also under question. Though they were all older women, none had a recent history of severe health issues, yet Shipman would claim they had died from serious illnesses. Winnie Mellor, an active and healthy woman in her early 70s, had supposedly died from a sudden heart attack. Two other women in their 70s had fallen victim to pneumonia, while a younger woman was struck with cancer. There was no proof of any of this.

Shipman had tried to cover his tracks regarding these fabricated illnesses by editing patient records. The computerized system he used allowed him to alter previous entries. This is where he claimed that Mellor had experienced chest pains and Mrs.

Grundy was a chronic drug user. He apparently had no idea that the date these changes were made was also logged by the system, and they were all recent. This was discovered by Detective Sergeant John Ashley, a computer expert.

All in all, the prosecution made incredibly compelling arguments, and a few months later, On January 31, 2000, Shipman was found guilty on all counts. He faced fifteen life sentences – with an addition of four more years for forging Mrs. Grundy's will.

His official list of confirmed victims:

Marie West (The earliest victim he was charged with)

Irene Turner (Whose mother was also murdered by Shipman)

Lizzie Adams (77, died February 28, 1997)

Jean Lilley

Ivy Lomas

Muriel Grimshaw (76, died July 1997)

Marie Quinn

Kathleen Wagstaff

Bianka Pomfret (Suffered from mental illness)

Norah Nuttall

Pamela Hillier (68, died February 9, 1998)

Maureen Ward (58, died February 18, 1998)

Winifred Mellor (The last of the victims to be exhumed)

Joan Melia

Kathleen Grundy

XI

The Doctor's Death

SHIPMAN WAS CONVICTED ON FEBRUARY 1, 2000, but it was not the end. Victims of the families and other locals demanded a further investigation into his crimes. This was granted in September of the same year. Dame Janet Smith would head the inquiry now known as The Shipman Inquiry, a lengthy report examining his crimes and what could have been done to prevent them.

This is where the purported number of two hundred-plus victims originated. At the start of the inquiry, there were nearly a thousand deaths that needed to be investigated, but soon the number was whittled down to the count the doctor is infamous for today. Almost forty thousand documents were scanned, and countless witnesses were interviewed. Today, the final report can be easily accessed by anyone through multiple websites online.

One thing that has seemingly never been conclusively answered is: why? Why did Shipman kill – and why so many? Did he get a thrill from murder? One thinks back to the afternoons of his youth spent beside his ailing mother. Did he believe that, in some twisted way, he was helping his patients?

Or was it for personal gain? After all, he had tried to falsely inherit the nearly four hundred thousand pound estate of Mrs. Grundy. On at least one occasion, it was believed that he stole jewelry from a victim's home. These, however, are in the minority of cases.

Unfortunately, we will never know the real truth. Shipman took it to his grave on the eve of his fifty-eighth birthday. In the early hours of January 13, 2004, he hung himself with bedsheets in his cell at HM Prison Wakefield when the guards were not looking.

His last known words to his wife when they talked on the phone were, "I love you, too. Don't forget, I will always look after you."

It was by killing himself that he ensured she could continue to receive his pension. He had lost it when convicted, but he found a loophole that made it so his family could receive it before he turned sixty.

He had been a model prisoner during his time there, having even saved the life of his cellmate when the other man attempted suicide, comforting him and mentoring him on the importance of life.

Ironic words coming from a man who stole so many.

Conclusion

HAROLD FREDRICK SHIPMAN MAY NOT HAVE the same notoriety outside of the United Kingdom as other serial killers. His story seems to lack the same drama, the same sort of blood and guts that gets people interested. He had no traumatic upbringing that molded him into the murderer he became. In this sense, he is something of an anomaly.

What else could make a person sink to such levels of depravity? He took hundreds of lives like it was nothing. Not once did he ever show any remorse or even admit that he was guilty of anything.

Shipman's story may not be scary for the reasons so many fear serial killers. Instead, he shows us that one does not need to have something "wrong" with them in order to become a bad person. The murderer with the highest kill count in the world had no history of mental illness aside from drug addiction.

It is no wonder he blended in so well with the regular world. At the end of the day, Harold Shipman was simply one of us.

References

"Harold Shipman's Clinical Practice" Retrieved from: https://murderpedia.org/male.S/images/shipman-harold/reports/shipman-clinical-practice.pdf

"Dr. Harold Frederick Shipman" Retrieved from: https://murderpedia.org/male.S/s/shipman-harold.htm

"Shipman's youngest victim identified as four-year-old girl murdered in hospital" Retrieved from: https://www.independent.co.uk/news/uk/crime/shipman-s-youngest-victim-identified-as-fouryearold-girl-murdered-in-hospital-488490.html

"Tragic story of how four-year-old Susie Garfitt became Harold Shipman's youngest victim" Retrieved from: https://www.dailystar.co.uk/tv/tragic-story-how-four-year-22754557

"I was with Dr Death when he started his killing, I feel sick we didn't stop him then." Retrieved from: https://www.thefreelibrary.com/I+was+with+Dr+Death+when+he+started+his+killing%2C+I+feel+sick+we...-a0129330436

"Nurse who worked with Harold Shipman 'haunted' for 30 years for not reporting three deaths on night shift together" Retrieved from:

https://www.mirror.co.uk/tv/tv-news/nurse-who-worked-harold-shipman-12427180

"What happened to Harold Shipman's wife, Primrose Shipman?" Retrieved from: https://www.tuko.co.ke/410115-what-happened-harold-shipmans-wife-primrose-shipman.html

"Kathleen's exhumation a first for police" Retrieved from: https://www.manchestereveningnews.co.uk/news/local-news/kathleens-exhumation-a-first-for-police-1182864

"GP came close to confessing, says ex-cellmate." Retrieved from: https://www.theguardian.com/society/2004/jan/15/NHS.shipman1#:~:text= The%20GP's%20former%20cellmate%20also,me%20I%20was%20safe%20now.

"The Shipman Inquiry." Retrieved from: https://webarchive.nationalarchives.gov.uk/ukgwa/20090808155005/http://www.the-shipman-inquiry.org.uk/home.asp

Green, R. (2015) *Harold Shipman – The True Story of Britain's Most Notorious Serial Killer* Ryan Green Publishing

White, D. (2016) *Harold Shipman: Dr Death* (True Crime Shorts Book 10)

Whittle, B. and Ritchie, J. (2000) *Harold Shipman: Prescription for Murder* Time Warner Books

Acknowledgements

This is a special thanks to the following readers who have taken time out of their busy schedule to be part of True Crime Seven Team. Thank you all so much for all the feedbacks and support!

Robert Upton, Angie Grafton, Alicia Gir, Anna Rohrbach, Ashlynn Stinson, Angela Brockman, Bambi Dawn Goggio, Casey Renee Bates, Kurt Brown, Barbara English, Kris Bowers, Cara Butcher, Joyce Carroll, Cory Lindsey, Deirdre Green, Clara Cortex, Nancy Harrison, Dannnii Desjarlais, David Edmonds, Debbie Hill, Debbie Gabriel, Diane, Larry J. Field, Linda J Evans, Huw, Jennifer Lloyd, Jennie, Jon Wiederhorn, Judy Stephens, Fran Joyner, Kay, Jennifer Jones, Laura Rouston, Jason, Michele Gosselin, Mark Sawyer, Monica Yokel, Marcia Heacock, Muhammad Nizam Bin Mohtar, Bonnie Kernene, Nicky McLean, Ole Pedersen, Kathy Morgan, Patricia Oliver, Rebecca Ednie, Robert Fritsch, Christy Riemenschneider, Shane Neely, Don Price, Tammy Sittlinger, Tina Bullard, Tina Shattuck, Tina Rattray-Green, Tamela L. Matuska, Marcie Walters, Wendy Lippard

Continue Your Exploration Into

The Murderous Minds

Excerpt From True Crime Storytime

Volume 1

I

Ruth Snyder and Henry Judd Gray

A tale of two lovers so captivating it was turned into a film. Ruth Snyder is played by the alluring Barbara Stanwyck and the charming Fred MacMurray as Henry Judd Gray. Though the 1944 crime noir movie attracted audiences and won the acclaim of critics, the real-life scenario was nothing to be praised.

Nevertheless, the true affair and murder did consume the public's thoughts and hold their interest for quite some time. A love so passionate the couple was willing to commit murder. It was scintillating.

Ruth and her lover would eventually meet the same fate, on the exact same day, death by electrocution. Their stories and lives are forever entangled. They would continue to capture the public's attention even beyond death.

A stolen photo of Snyder's last moments, taken by a camera hidden in the pant leg of a newspaperman, was run on the front page of the Daily News. The issue sold out in just fifteen minutes.

The pair, which the movie *Double Indemnity* was based on, wanted anything but notoriety; however, they achieved it in spades.

A Housewife From Queens

New York City in the Jazz Age. The setting of the Great Gatsby, home to gangsters and speakeasies, a playground for the rich and famous. Well, at least in the wealthier parts of the city.

The population of Queens nearly doubled in the 1920s. The subway system expanded, the automobile grew increasingly popular, and newly-built bridges made the borough much more accessible.

For some families, like the Snyder's, an address in the Queens neighborhood was a move up in life. You were on your way, one step closer to the parties, the wealth, the celebrities. Unfortunately, Ruth Snyder didn't share her husband's sentiments and this was the beginning of the end. Mr. Snyder's final scene would close with him being bludgeoned, suffocated with chloroform-soaked cotton, and strangled with picture frame wire.

Ruth Snyder was born Ruth Brown in 1895. Where she would eventually find herself living with her husband and daughter wasn't too far from her place of birth, 125th Street, Manhattan. Her Scandinavian parents were average and of the working class. Like many immigrants of the time, they got by and that was enough.

But Ruth had higher aspirations. She completed the eighth grade and then left school. Forsaking a formal education for a job with a telephone company. At night she took classes in both shorthand and typing. While she was a hard worker and one would believe she was determined to make a living for herself as a single woman, Ruth said she always "thought more of marriage than [of] a business career."

Little did she know, her ticket to success was closer than she could have imagined. At nineteen, Motor Boating Magazine offered her a secretarial position. Ruth was dedicated but she was also spunky and lively, described as "gay" and "fun-loving." A product of the 1920s, she possessed the energetic freedom and sometimes risky behaviors of her feminist peers, the flappers of the Jazz Age.

It is no surprise then that the magazine's art editor, Albert Snyder, was intrigued by the company's new sassy secretary. At thirty-two, he was thirteen years Ruth's senior, but she didn't mind his attention in the least.

She had far less experience than Albert in the romance department, a fact that may have contributed to the events to come. Albert was Ruth's first true "gentleman friend," and after courting for a few months they were engaged and shortly thereafter married.

At twenty years old, Ruth was now a housewife. It would be three more years before she was a model Queens housewife, the envy of her fellow secretaries.

Ruth's aspirations of being a businesswoman slowly faded away. She was preoccupied with taking care of the home, then she became a mother. The couple named their daughter Lorraine and needing a bigger space, upgraded to a larger Bronx apartment.

Albert was successful at the magazine and was soon able to surprise his wife and child with an impressive eight-room home in Queens Village on Long Island. The Snyder family had finally arrived. Only, for Ruth, the ticket was to a lonely suburban life of cleaning, cooking, mending, and caring for her daughter.

Lonely and Looking for Love

Friends and acquaintances would eventually tell the papers that by 1925, Ruth possessed "everything that most women wish for." Meaning, a house, an automobile, a radio, good furniture, money in the bank, protection, and an athlete for a husband. Albert was a good man and a faithful husband. He took pride in his wife, his child, and his home. He made little things to decorate the house and he was thrifty, but he also worked hard and late.

Sadly, friends and family failed to see that this model husband was also evil-tempered and pessimistic. Ruth's mother got a glimpse behind the rosy curtain when she moved in with Ruth and Albert. Her daughter loved to go out, was cheerful, and sociable while her son-in-law was gloomy, a homebody, and generally uninterested in anything Ruth was.

What's more, Albert never wanted children and the fact that their only offspring was a girl was a difficult blow. To say that Ruth and Albert were not well-suited would be an understatement.

Ruth's mom would often overhear Albert telling Ruth how he wished she was more like his previous fiancée, Jessie Guischard, who passed away before they were to be married. If only Ruth could be more serious like her.

Ruth's mother advised her to seek a divorce, instead, Ruth sought a lover.

A tall, blonde woman with a captivating personality, it wasn't hard for Ruth to find a beau. She met a married, corset salesman named Henry Judd Gray at lunch one day. Another man her polar opposite, Henry was short, unremarkable, and quiet. Yet the pair got along fabulously and soon took up a passionate affair.

Albert worked at the magazine during the day and Lorraine, now nine, was in school. On the unfortunate occasions when Lorraine had a holiday, Ruth would leave her in a hotel lobby and sneak to a room upstairs with Henry. The couple was insatiable.

It is hard to say exactly when Ruth crossed from madly in love with another man to murderous. She was bored in her life, and she fought frequently with her husband. Maybe she was looking for excitement and a thrill. Maybe she saw a clear path out of a broken marriage, a plan too fail-proof to pass up. Whatever the case, she probably should've heeded her mother's advice about legally ending her marriage before turning to murder.

Murder for Momsie?

Ruth and Henry had pet names for each other; he was called "Lover Boy" and she "Momsie." When Ruth had made up her mind that her husband had to go, she began to work on warming Henry up to the idea of murder.

At first, she started with hints that Albert mistreated her, then she resorted to persistently nagging him and suggesting that he help her commit the crime. She slowly wore Henry down, though he was so adverse to the idea he took to drinking heavily.

When Ruth had resorted to begging, threatening, and finally demanding that Henry commit murder for Momsie, he gave in. The pair devised a plan.

Ruthless Ruth

Henry would take the train from Syracuse to New York, then he would hop a bus to Long Island and finally arrive in Queens. Henry's old pal, Haddon Gray, agreed to assist with an alibi under the pretense that Henry was going to visit a girlfriend.

In order to dupe Henry's wife, Haddon posted two letters to her in Henry's name, mussed his hotel bed sheets, and hung a "Do Not Disturb" sign on his door. As far as anyone knew, Henry was still in Syracuse. However, he was up to something much more sinister than visiting a girlfriend a few towns over.

On Saturday, March 19, 1927, witnesses would recall that Henry seemingly wanted to be caught. He was spotted walking around Ruth's neighborhood, drinking from a flask in broad daylight; begging for prohibition police to arrest him before he could carry out his lover's dark deed.

But alas he wasn't arrested, at least not yet. He quietly slipped into Ruth's unoccupied home and waited in a spare room for the family to return from a party. Ruth had stocked the room with all the homicidal necessities: a window weight, rubber gloves, and chloroform.

When the family returned around two in the morning, Albert and the couple's daughter quickly retired. Ruth went to visit "Lover Boy" for one last romp before they carried out their nefarious plan. After nearly an hour, the pair snuck into the master bedroom, Henry carrying the window sash weight.

When they arrived they found Albert sleeping deeply, his form completely covered by the blankets. Ruth stood on one side of the bed and Henry on the other. Henry raised the window weight, preparing to bring it down on the unsuspecting husband's head.

Whether it was subconscious reluctance or lack of experience, the weight merely glanced off Albert's skull. Enough to wake him but not do any real damage. He arose from the bed stunned but enraged, furiously trying to fight off his attacker.

Timid and terrified Henry shouted, "Momsie, Momsie, for God's sake, help!" Ruth was unphased. She let out a grunt of disgust, realizing her lover was too weak to finish the deed and she would have to take matters into her own hands.

With steady fists she swiftly seized the weight and bludgeoned her husband's skull, killing him almost instantly. But just to be sure, the pair shoved chloroform-soaked cotton balls up his nose and strangled him with picture frame wire.

That's where the couple's plan ended. What did they do now? With Ruth's daughter Lorraine blissfully unaware of the recent events, she and Henry went downstairs for a nightcap and to discuss the missing details of their plan.

They decided to stage a robbery. They scattered some papers here, flipped over a few chairs there, and finally hid a few objects that Ruth would later claim as stolen. Henry then loosely bound Ruth's hands and feet and slipped away into the night.

Lorraine was awoken by her mother, tied at the wrists and ankles, banging on her door. She ran to the neighbors to phone the police.

A Bad Breakup

The police were suspicious from the beginning, especially because the gruesomeness of Albert's murder wasn't consistent with typical break-ins. None of the signs pointed to robbery, and the most damning evidence was the fact that all of the items Ruth claimed were stolen, the police were able to locate in the Snyder residence. Her missing jewelry was recovered from under her very own mattress.

They turned up Ruth's address book with the names of twenty-eight men, the window weight used to bludgeon Albert was found in the basement, and finally in the master bedroom a small pin. It was emblazoned with the initials J.G. for Jessie Guischard.

Albert was never without the token from his former fl.

but police matched the J.G. to a name in the recovered addres

book — "Judd Gray." A pin likely dropped by the murderer corresponding to a name in the vengeful wife's address book? An unlikely coincidence.

When the police asked Ruth about Henry Judd Gray she asked, "Has he confessed?" Yes, he had the police told her. For reasons unknown, Ruth told the truth or at least a half-truth. She admitted to conspiring with Henry but claimed it was him who ultimately dealt the death blow.

Henry was found just a few short hours later, holed up in his hotel room. He put up a bit more of a front than Ruth, asserting his innocence and saying he was nowhere near the city. Until police presented the train ticket stub found in his hotel trash can. He confessed, blaming the whole messy murder on Ruth.

The nail in the coffin for the pair was a double-indemnity insurance policy Ruth had taken out in Albert's name for nearly one hundred thousand dollars in the event of his accidental death, just before his grisly murder.

The Dumbbell Murder Case

By the time the trial arrived for Henry and Ruth, the former lovers were more than spiteful. They each had separate lawyers proclaiming their innocence and declaring the guilt of the other. While sensational, the trial became known as the dumbbell murder case, for how dumb the whole poorly planned homicide was.

Henry claimed Ruth hypnotized and seduced him, convincing him to murder her abusive husband. Ruth stated that Albert "drove love out of the house" and that Henry assisted her in setting up the insurance policy to tempt her. In fact, Henry regularly took her to speakeasies, tried to convince her to smoke, and even once sent her poison to murder her husband. Henry was the bad influence while she was a pious homemaker, reading the Bible to her daughter and attending church on Sundays.

The media had a field day. Celebrities attended the trial, famous reporters worked overtime, and the authorities and medical coroners were running back and forth testifying in both ongoing trials. The ordeal became one of the top media events of the 1920s. The adultery and subsequent murder proclaimed a "cancer in the city" that was the epitome of many immoral behaviors taking place as of late.

The two former lovers would be made an example and authorities stated, they would "excise this social cancer and re-establish the old standards." The tabloids took a different stance. Detailing every forbidden touch, meeting, and behavior. Allowing the public to indulge in a buffet of voyeurism.

By the end of the trial, two things were apparent: the masses couldn't get enough of the thought of sneaking away to a hotel for a mid-day hour of clandestine sex and respectable women did not smoke, drink, dye their hair, cross their legs, lunch out with strange men, or feel ingratitude toward their husbands.

Ruth and Henry may appear ordinary, but they were not, said the authorities. By the end of the trial, Ruth had been made out to be barely a human, much less a lady. She was referred to as "The Granite Woman," "Vampire Wife," or "Ruthless Ruth."

This may have made it easier for the jury to deliver their verdict of guilty and to receive death by electrocution. And Henry? He was just a "poor boob" duped by a woman and unable to stand up for his morals. He received a guilty verdict as well, receiving the same fate as his ex-lover.

Henry and Ruth were executed on the same day, January 12, 1928.

Henry was said to be calm and of a clear conscience, having received a letter of forgiveness from his wife.

Ruth was electrocuted moments later. Her final thoughts making it clear she had learned the lesson the public so desperately wanted to teach her. She said, "If I were to live over again, I would be what I want my child to be—a good girl, really making the fear of God a guide to a straight life."

About True Crime Seven

True Crime Seven is about exploring the stories of the sinful minds in this world. From unknown murderers to well-known serial killers.

Our writers come from all walks of life but with one thing in common and that is they are all true crime enthusiasts. You can learn more about them below:

Ryan Becker is a True Crime author who started his writing journey in late 2016. Like most of you, he loves to explore the process of how individuals turn their darkest fantasies into a reality. Ryan has always had a passion for storytelling. So, writing is the best output for him to combine his fascination with psychology and true crime. It is Ryan's goal for his readers to experience the full immersion with the dark reality of the world just like how he used to do it in his younger days.

Nancy Alyssa Veysey is a writer and author of true crime books, including the bestselling, Mary Flora Bell: The Horrific True Story Behind an Innocent Girl Serial Killer. Her medical degree and work in the field of forensic psychology, along with postgraduate studies in criminal justice, criminology and pre-law, allow her to bring a unique perspective to her writing.

Kurtis-Giles Veysey is a young writer who began his writing career in the fantasy genre. In late 2018, he has parlayed his love and knowledge of history into writing nonfiction accounts of true crime stories which occurred in centuries past. Told from a historical perspective, Kurtis-Giles brings these victims and their killers back to life with vivid descriptions of these heinous crimes.

Kelly Gaines is a writer from Philadelphia. Her passion for storytelling began in childhood and carried into her college career. She received a B.A. in English from Saint Joseph's University in 2016 with a concentration in Writing Studies. Now part of the real world, Kelly enjoys comic books, history documentaries, and a good scary story. In her true crime work, Kelly focuses on the motivations of the killers and backgrounds of the victims to draw a more complete picture of each individual. She deeply enjoys writing for True Crime Seven and looks forward to bringing more spine-tingling tales to readers.

James Parker the pen-name of a young writer from New Jersey who started his writing journey with play-writing. He has always been fascinated with the psychology of murderers and how the media might play a role in their creation. James loves to constantly test out new styles and ideas in his writing so one day he can find something cool and unique to himself.

Brenda Brown is a writer and an illustrator-cartoonist. Her art can be found in books distributed both nationally and internationally. She has also written many books related to her graduate degree in psychology and her minor in history. Like many true crime enthusiasts, she loves exploring the minds of those who see the world as a playground for expressing the darker side of themselves—the side that people usually locked up and hid from scrutiny.

Genoveva Ortiz is a Los Angeles-based writer who began her career writing scary stories while still in college. After receiving a B.A. in English in 2018, she shifted her focus to nonfiction and the real-life horrors of crime and unsolved mysteries. Together with True Crime Seven, she is excited to further explore the world of true crime through a social justice perspective.

You can learn more about us and our writers at:

truecrimeseven.com/about

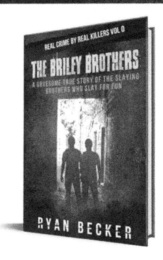

Dark Fantasies Turned Reality

Prepare yourself, we're not going to **hold back on details or cut out any of the gruesome truths...**

Made in the USA
Las Vegas, NV
30 October 2022

58433543R00079